NOTE TO PARENTS

Apologetics Press is a non-profit organization dedicated to the defense of New Testament Christianity. For over 35 years, we have provided faith-building materials for adults. We also have produced numerous products (*Discovery* magazine, our *Explorer Series*, children's tracts, *Digger Doug's Underground* DVDs, and various books) for young people from infancy through high school. The A.P. readers are some of our most popular children's materials.

The Apologetics Press Advanced Reader Series is a step up from our Early Reader Series. The Advanced Reader Series is aimed at children in 2nd-3rd grades. Although our Advanced Readers have about the same number of pages as our Early Readers, the Advanced Readers have twice as much text, as well as more advanced words.

With beautiful, full-color pictures and interesting facts about God's wonderfully designed Creation, your children will develop a greater love for reading and for their grand Designer.

We hope you enjoy using the Apologetics Press Advanced Reader Series to encourage your children to read, while at the same time helping them learn about God and His Creation.

See also our Learn to Read Series
for 3-6 year olds and our
Early Reader Series for K-2nd graders
ApologeticsPress.org
(800) 234-8558

Amazing Dinosaurs, Designed by God

by Kyle Butt

© 2009 Apologetics Press, Inc.

ISBN-13: 978-1-60063-015-6
Library of Congress: 2009905909

Layout and design: Rob Baker
Illustrator: Lewis Lavoie
Printed in China

APOLOGETICS PRESS, INC.
230 LANDMARK DRIVE
MONTGOMERY, AL 36117-2752

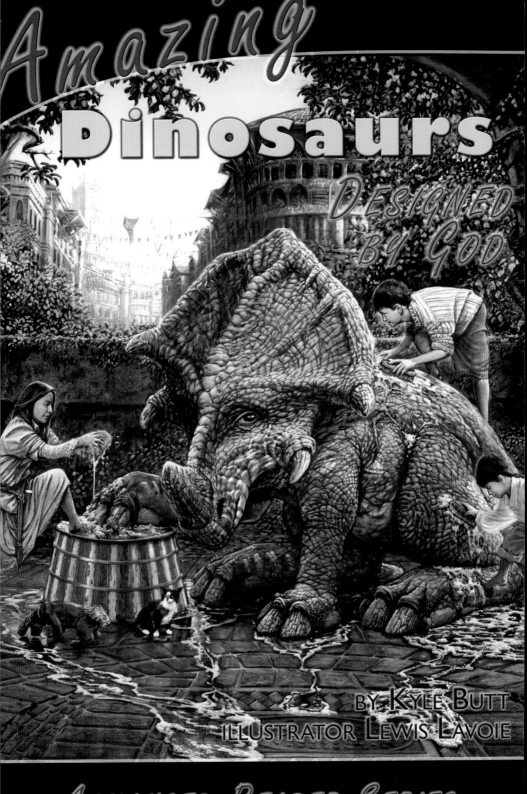

Amazing
Dinosaurs

DESIGNED BY GOD

BY KYLE BUTT

ILLUSTRATOR LEWIS LAVOIE

ADVANCED READER SERIES

God made all the different kinds of animals on days five and six of the Creation week. He made birds, bears, horses, and beetles. But there is one group of animals that people sometimes forget God made during Creation. These animals are called dinosaurs. The word "dinosaur" means "terribly great lizard." God created dinosaurs on day six of Creation.

Some people teach things about dinosaurs that are not right. Some scientists teach that God did not create dinosaurs. They teach that dinosaurs evolved. These people also teach that dinosaurs lived millions of years before humans lived. That is not right.

The Bible says that God made everything in six days. That means He made dinosaurs during the Creation. The Bible also says that God made humans on the sixth day of Creation. Day six of Creation is the same day God made animals that walk on the Earth.

Dinosaurs are animals that walked on the Earth. That means God made them on day six. They did not evolve millions of years before humans were on the Earth. They were created on the same day that God made Adam and Eve. In fact, the Bible says that Adam named all the animals. Adam saw dinosaurs and even named them.

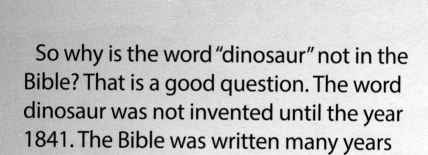

So why is the word "dinosaur" not in the Bible? That is a good question. The word dinosaur was not invented until the year 1841. The Bible was written many years before that.

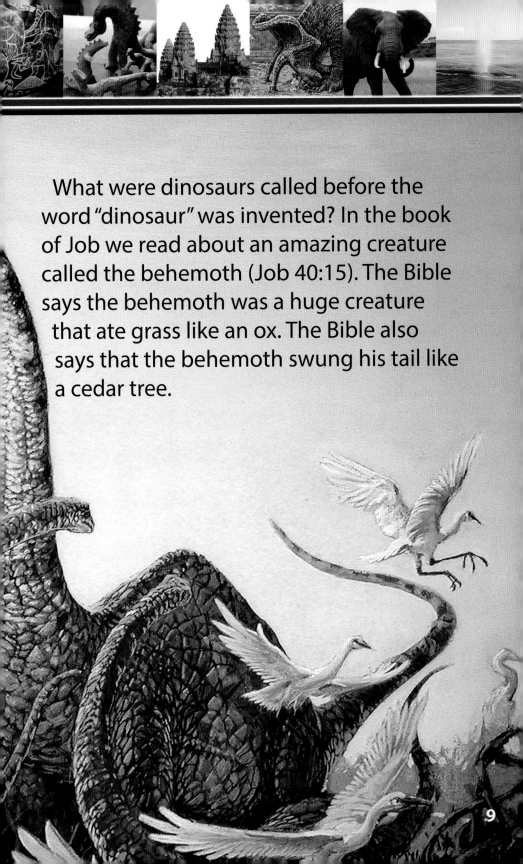

What were dinosaurs called before the word "dinosaur" was invented? In the book of Job we read about an amazing creature called the behemoth (Job 40:15). The Bible says the behemoth was a huge creature that ate grass like an ox. The Bible also says that the behemoth swung his tail like a cedar tree.

The Bible's description of this creature sounds exactly like a dinosaur. Some people try to say that the behemoth was an elephant or a hippo. But when you look at the tails of elephants and hippos, you know that cannot be right.

Elephants and hippos have tiny tails. They do not have long, thick tails like a cedar tree. They have tails like little sticks. Huge plant-eating dinosaurs match the traits of behemoth much better than an elephant or a hippo.

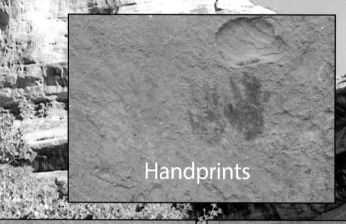

Handprints

Goat (ibex)

Human

The Bible says that humans and dinosaurs have lived together from the beginning of Creation. We know that humans who lived in the past saw dinosaurs. People in the past drew pictures of dinosaurs. We see these pictures all over the world.

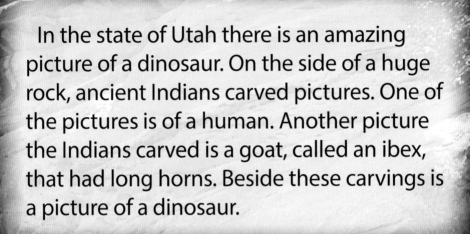

   In the state of Utah there is an amazing picture of a dinosaur. On the side of a huge rock, ancient Indians carved pictures. One of the pictures is of a human. Another picture the Indians carved is a goat, called an ibex, that had long horns. Beside these carvings is a picture of a dinosaur.

Do you see the dinosaur's long neck and tail?

The dinosaur that the Indians drew is a large dinosaur that ate plants. Fossils of a dinosaur just like the one on the rock were found close to the carving. That means the dinosaur lived in the area. And it means that the Indians could have seen the huge creature.

People who believe in evolution do not believe that humans ever saw dinosaurs. But they cannot deny that the carving looks just like a dinosaur. If people really did live with dinosaurs, the carving on the rock is just what we would expect to find.

Ancient people left many other pictures of dinosaurs. Thousands of stones have been found in the country of Peru. These stones have carvings of people and animals on them. Many of the animals are dinosaurs.

Many of the carvings on the stones show people and dinosaurs together. Some of the

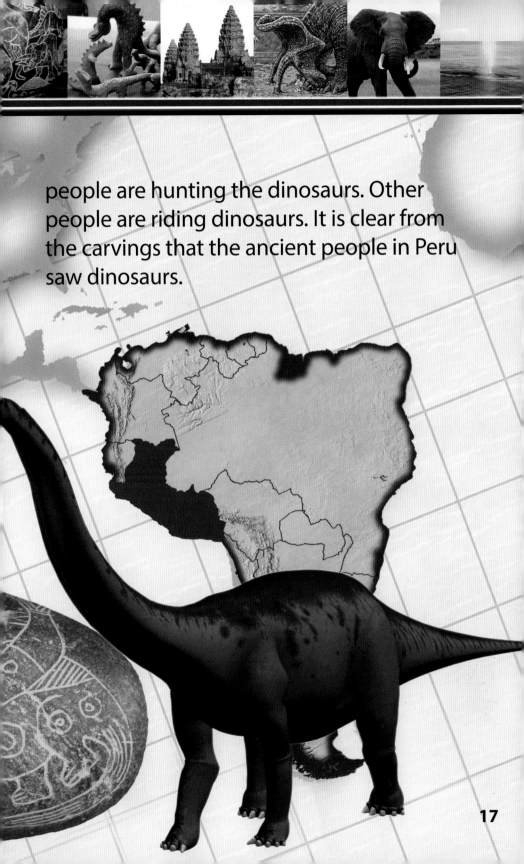

people are hunting the dinosaurs. Other people are riding dinosaurs. It is clear from the carvings that the ancient people in Peru saw dinosaurs.

Many of the dinosaurs carved on the stones are plant-eating dinosaurs. They are carved with pointy spikes on their backs. In modern times, scientists did not know that these long-necked dinosaurs had pointy spikes until the year 1992. But the stones were carved many years before 1992. How could the people in Peru have known that the dinosaurs had pointy spikes? These stones show that ancient people must have seen the dinosaurs.

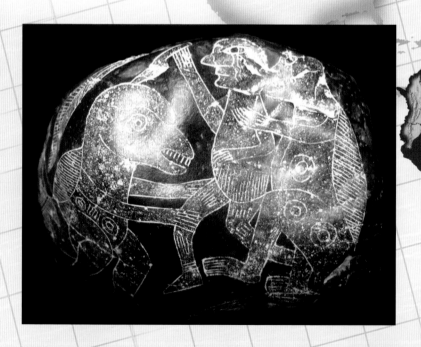

Images courtesy of www.Bible.ca

If God created dinosaurs on the same day as humans, carvings like those on the Ica stones are just what we would expect to find. Not only do these ancient carvings prove that humans saw dinosaurs, they also help to show that dinosaurs did not evolve.

In the 1940s, a man in Mexico found thousands of clay figurines. The clay figures were very old. Many of them were buried deep in the ground. Some of the clay figures are of animals and people. Many of the animals are still alive today, like small lizards and anteaters. But some of the clay figures are statues of dinosaurs.

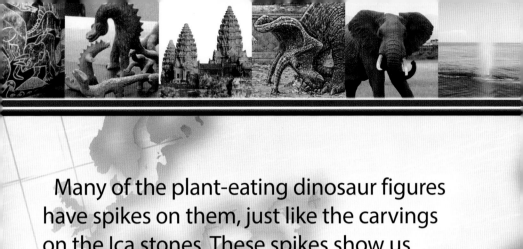

Many of the plant-eating dinosaur figures have spikes on them, just like the carvings on the Ica stones. These spikes show us that whoever carved the stones knew more about dinosaurs than modern people knew until the year 1992.

Images courtesy of www.Bible.ca

Another carving of a dinosaur is found in the country of Cambodia. Hundreds of years ago a king built a big temple. In that temple, many kinds of animals were carved on the walls. On one wall there are carvings of parrots, a monkey, and a deer. On that same wall is a carving of a dinosaur called a *Stegasaurus* [steh-guh-SORE-us]. The carving was made hundreds of years before modern people started finding dinosaur bones.

Images courtesy of www.Bible.ca

The people who built the temple must have known what a *Stegasaurus* looked like. How would they have known this? The best answer is that they **saw** a *Stegasaurus*. If they saw this dinosaur, then we know that dinosaurs did not become extinct millions of years before humans lived on the Earth.

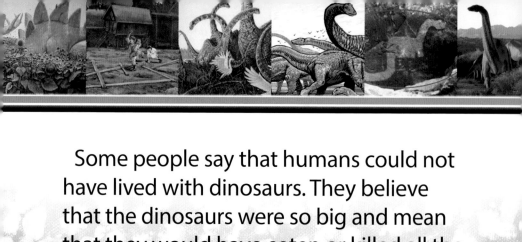

Some people say that humans could not have lived with dinosaurs. They believe that the dinosaurs were so big and mean that they would have eaten or killed all the people. But that is not right. God created humans to be much smarter than animals.

God gave humans the ability to control and tame animals. In fact, humans can control the largest land animals in the world—elephants.

Elephants can weigh 22,000 pounds. That is bigger than most trucks, and bigger than many of the dinosaurs. An elephant could easily step on a person and kill him. Yet humans have trained huge elephants to do many tricks. Humans have also tamed many meat-eating animals.

The killer whale can weigh 10,000 pounds. It has a mouth full of very sharp teeth. But humans can swim with killer whales and teach them tricks.

Humans can tame other animals like lions, tigers, and bears. The blue whale is the biggest animal that has ever lived, as far as we know. It is bigger than any dinosaur. Yet humans in the past hunted the blue whale and killed many of them.

Some dinosaurs were very big. But others were very small. The average size of dinosaurs was only about the size of a cow. Humans easily could have lived with dinosaurs without being killed by them.

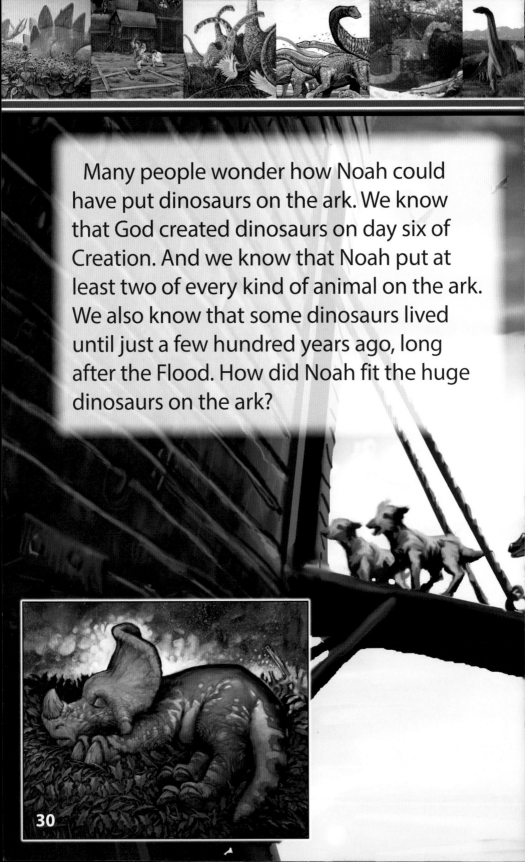

Many people wonder how Noah could have put dinosaurs on the ark. We know that God created dinosaurs on day six of Creation. And we know that Noah put at least two of every kind of animal on the ark. We also know that some dinosaurs lived until just a few hundred years ago, long after the Flood. How did Noah fit the huge dinosaurs on the ark?

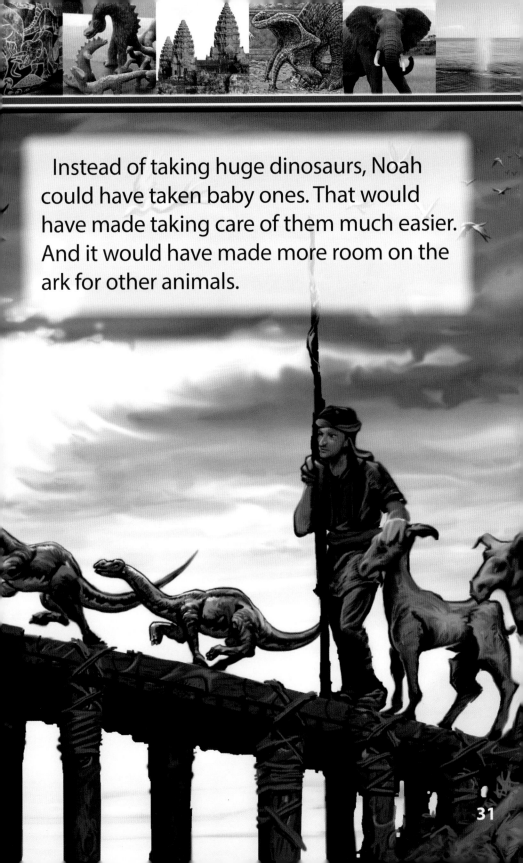

Instead of taking huge dinosaurs, Noah could have taken baby ones. That would have made taking care of them much easier. And it would have made more room on the ark for other animals.

God created dinosaurs on the same day of Creation that He made humans. Humans saw dinosaurs, drew pictures of them, and told stories about them. The Bible also describes a creature called the behemoth that sounds much like a huge, plant-eating dinosaur. Dinosaurs were not separated from humans by millions of years. God created them both together.